©Consafos Press
PO Box 931568, LA CA 90093 USA www.consafospress.com

Written by Andrew Kidman and Andy Davis copyright ©2002
Photography by Andrew Kidman~ www.litmus.com.au
Illustrations by Andy Davis~ .andoland.net & andofromorlando.com

First Published 2004 by Consafos Press
ISBN 0965653595
All rights reserved. No part of this book may be reproduced, transmitted, sampled or stored in any form digital or otherwise, without the written permission of the Publisher.

Typographic design: Michele Lockwood
Computer Graphics: Neal Purchase, Jr.
Layout: Neal Purchase

Printed in Singapore by Americanbook.net

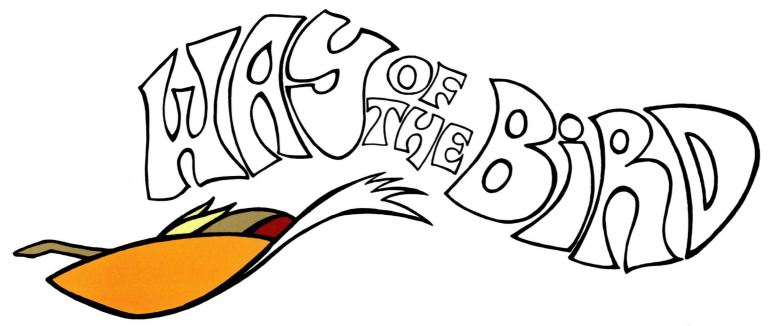

By Andrew Kidman & Andy Davis

For Skip, Mish, Bella Love, Ashley and Noah Nakima

The boy found himself at the beach staring out to sea. The waves that washed ashore captivated him. They had no reason nor meaning but they kept coming, one after the other. Rising to the sky, and filling the air with their shapes, color and beauty.

As the waves came crashing down they made a sound he'd never heard before, like rumbling thunder in the night.

Suddenly a man appeared riding a wave on what looked to be a piece of wood.

The man glided across the waves like a bird through the sky.
The boy watched in wonder as the man rode each wave to shore, then paddled back out to sea to catch another ride. He did this over and over again. The boy was mesmerized by the man's dance. Time stood still for the boy as he sat lost in his new discovery.

The sun dipped into the ocean as the boy noticed the man's board being washed ashore.

The boy ran down and picked the board up from where it lay on the shoreline. The board was heavy. It was the most beautiful thing he'd ever laid eyes on. It was made from some kind of strange wood, the grain illuminated in the sun's final rays.
"That's balsa wood," said the man.

    The boy turned and looked at him. He was shocked by the man's old age; his gray matted hair and leathered skin. The boy could not believe it was the same man he'd been watching for hours.

    Then he looked into his eyes.

The old man's eyes were deep like the sea and they sparkled like the sun's light on the waves he'd seen earlier. They were alive with life like the eyes of a child.

"What are you doing?" asked the inquisitive boy.

"Surfing," said the man. "Would you like to try it?"

"Yes I would." said the boy excitedly.

The man paddled the boy out into the ocean.

The water was alive and seemingly moving the boy around with a will of it's own. The presence of the man calmed him. He felt safe and at home in the surf, a feeling he'd never felt before.
"Here comes a wave. Hold onto the board, I'll push you onto it." yelled the man.

    The swell lifted the boy into the air as the man pushed him down the face of the wave. He gripped the rails of the board and held on for his life. He felt like he was flying over the water at a great speed. As the fin of the board caught in the shallow shoreline the boy was overcome with feelings of joy. He screamed with delight.

Turning back to the sea he saw the man riding a wave to shore on his stomach. Once again he saw the grace of the bird. The man walked up to the boy, they were both smiling, the boy stood speechless.

"Doesn't get any better than that." said the man.

They turned and walked up the beach together. The boy had so many questions he wanted to ask the man.

That night the boy couldn't sleep. His mind was filled with visions of things he was going to do in the ocean. He wanted to ride waves like the man. He felt like he'd found a purpose for his life; he was going to be a surfer.

The next morning the boy returned to the beach to find the man waiting for him.
"I knew I'd find you here." said the man. He pulled an old board from the back of his truck and handed it to the boy.
"This was my first board and now it's yours."
The boy ran his hands over the rails, smiling in anticipation.
"Come on, let's go ride some waves."

They had a wonderful first session together. The boy's favorite thing was to dive under the waves and watch the old man streak past in the tube.

The boy progressed quickly. He was naturally gifted in the ocean. He began riding bigger and more challenging surf. One day the surf was bigger and hollower than he'd ever ridden. From the shoulder he watched the old man pulling inside the waves with grace. He'd never seen such rides. His heart was pumping with adrenalin. He wanted more than anything to ride one of those waves.

He paddled into the take-off spot and sat with the man.

"Are you ready for one of these?" the man said.

"I think I am." said the boy.

"When the wave's upon you, don't hesitate." said the man.

A set came in and the boy began to paddle. The wave sucked fast on the reef and pulled the boy out of position. He stopped paddling and the old man swung around, took off and slipped easily into the barrel.

A bigger set approached, the boy was determined to ride one. He paddled hard into the belly of the wave. As the boy began to stand the wave lifted him up, but his board was too small for all the water in the wave. He wiped out - the lip launching him into space.

The wave sucked him over the falls and under the water. He felt like a rag doll in a washing machine. He was powerless against the waves force. Eventually the wave let him go and he broke the surface for air. He looked over and saw the old man laughing.
"I think it's time we made you a new board." he said.

That afternoon the boy went around to the man's house. The man was in the backyard looking over lengths of timber.

"This is going to be your new board." he said. The boy walked over and picked up one of the pieces of wood.

"Wow! It's light." said the boy.

"Light and strong which is what you want." said the man. "A board to last a lifetime. The first surfers made their boards out of trees they found in the forest." The man showed the boy a picture of Duke Kahanamoku surfing his giant redwood surfboard.

"Who was Duke Kahanamoku?" said the boy.

"He was a Hawaiian king, the world's greatest swimmer and he gave the gift of surfing to the world."

The man said. "Remember, that's what surfing is – a gift. Never take it for granted. Respect the ocean. It's creatures and others that play in it. For as easy as a gift is given it can be taken away."
"Just like you gave it to me." said the boy. The man smiled.
"This board we are going to build is like no other board. Most boards are made from foam, but that's not my trip. Foam is too disposable and it's terrible for the environment. Balsa is good because it carries the boards' momentum through the water. It also looks beautiful, it's a work of art."
"How do you make a surfboard out of a tree?" asked the boy.
"Well there's a secret to that. It's in my back pocket." said the man. He pulled a tattered piece of paper from his pocket and showed it to the boy. "A friend who taught me about surfing gave this to me."

Over the next week the man and the boy brought the wood to life. The man used skills the boy had never seen used anywhere else in life. The boy couldn't wait to get the board in the water.

The next morning the boy was at the beach at sunrise. He'd never been so excited in his whole life. He waxed his new board carefully, looking at the grain of the wood, feeling the curves, and imagining the lines he would draw with it on the waves.

The board was beautiful: a seven foot, single fin, pintail gun. As he carried the board into the water he was filled with joy. He baptized it in the shore-break and paddled it out.

As he made his way out through the waves another surfer came racing towards him. The surfer launched his board off the wave and into the air. The boy froze in amazement as the surfer crash landed on top of him.

They surfaced together, the surfer shouting at the boy.
"Stay out of my way kook!" he yelled. "What's that piece of junk you're riding? Get out of the water, you've got no right to be here."

The boy was stunned. He'd never experienced anything like this before in surfing. He couldn't understand how something so beautiful could be so ugly.

As he made his way up the beach he noticed a hole in his board. He sat in the sand. He was almost in tears when he felt a hand on his shoulder.
"No worries, we can fix it." said the old man.

They took the board back to the house. The boy was confused and full of questions.

"What kind of board was that other surfer riding? How did he fly up in the air like that? Why was he so upset with me?"

The man spoke to the boy gently.

"Surfing means different things to different people. I ride a board like this because of the way it paddles, the way it turns off the bottom, the speed it generates going down the line, and the way it holds in the tube. Also there will come a day when the surf's so big there is no other board that will handle the conditions. As far as that other surfer's attitude in the water, it has no place in surfing and is not in the spirit of the Duke. Remember surfing is a gift. Personally, I'd prefer to leave flying to the birds."

The old man smiled at the boy and patted him on the back.

"Let's fix this board and get you back in the water."

The boy was back in the water the next day. It was a magic board and he evolved into a great surfer. The board did everything the man said it would.

It paddled well and took the drop with ease.

t swung off the bottom with speed and power.

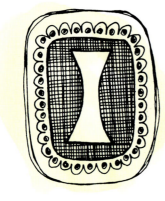t back-doored the tube with no loss of momentum, and carried smoothly over foam balls.

t put him inside places in nature he could never have imagined.

t shot from the tube like an arrow from a bow into the high line drive.

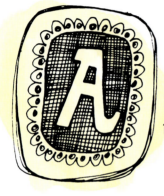nd it harnessed the speed of the wave as it cutback to the source.

For years the man and the boy surfed together, sharing the waves and experiences of the ocean. Just like the birds of the sea.

Then came a giant swell. The man and the boy watched it build through the day. In the evening they sat on the point following each huge wave with their eyes. It was a breathtaking sight. The offshore winds whipped the moving mountains, filling the air with watery horsetails. The man and the boy were pumped with adrenalin.

"Tomorrow is the day." said the man.

"I can't wait." said the boy.

The following day the waves were enormous. Everywhere was closed out.
"It's too big to ride." said the boy.
The man just smiled and said: "I know a place."

The man took the boy to his favorite secret spot. The waves were massive, without a drop of water out of place. The man and the boy shared the greatest session of their lives.

They rode the set of the day together, hooting from the take-off, screaming down the giant blue face. They kicked out in the channel, shaking their heads in disbelief. It was a magical day of days.

Life moved on after the big day. The boy became a man, and his old friend passed away. He continued surfing, keeping alive the lessons and spirit his friend had given him. He felt blessed to be a surfer and to experience all it was.

One morning while surfing alone he took off on a peeling wall. As he trimmed down the line a bird joined him for the ride. He watched the bird as it glided with the swell. It's grace was magnificent. The bird stalled on the wind and looked him in the eye.
The man smiled. Riding with the bird was just like surfing with his old friend.